The Testament of Enoch: A Pocketbook Edition to The Enochian Bible

YSL Enochial

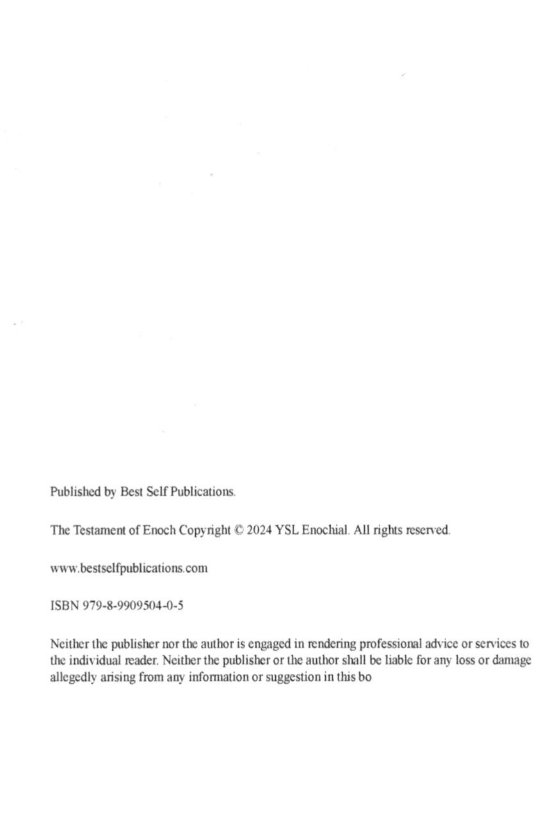

Published by Best Self Publications.

www.bestselfpublications.com

ISBN 979-8-9909504-0-5

Special praise be to Kamari Lord Havek, the sacred vessel of Enoch… for through you, all life sprang forth. You invoked the spirit of our Enochian ways… without you, we would have no physical presence.

To you, we dedicate this first edition, with all its glory, for you knew from the beginning that THIS would BECOME. And now here we are.

Let us commune… my old friend.

Hail Enoch! Praise by to the 63rd order!

Table of Contents

Introduction

This manual is NOT for those who are unfamiliar to the teachings of the infernal mysteries or for those who are not initiated into the egregor of Enochian Light. Newcomers may feel free to learn of our beliefs and contact the Lighthouse through the information in the back of this book. This manual has been compiled for the followers to better assist with the synchronization of the circle. Other books contain the history and metaphysical aspects of Enoch, Hermes, and Thoth - but this manual is specifically for the Chosen, the initiates to our Chain of Magic - each individual link. Enoch has provided his Chosen Elect and their students with accurate teachings and the healthy, correct way of life - a way that brings peace to the world and freedom to all. As with everything else, utopia is an uphill journey, one that the majority of mankind has not reached the level of spiritual maturity required to travel, blinding them from seeing the potential reality of beautiful world peace. Thus, Enoch has delivered his message to "those who can hear."

Testament of Enoch
scribed April 30, 2002
by the Standing One

Book One:

1. Before you, others have come,
   After you others will come.
2. Nothing in life is permanent.
3. What we rise, must fall.
4. What falls will rise again.
5. Change is the only constant,
   All else is illusion.
6. Leave your mark for others to find;
   as did those before you,
   so that those who come after will have light to guide them.
   And they will leave their mark for those who follow.
7. Blessed be the lineage.
8. Live your life as if the eyes of power can see your every action,
   as if a god is watching.
   Because watching, they are,
   and by your actions will you be judged.
9. Make your life an act of righteousness,
   an ongoing ritual,

following the path of the elders and ancestors, for they are self.

10. Respect your mother, Respect your father, Respect your elders, and Respect your culture;
11. but trust and rely upon your developed insight and experience
    before making decisions.
12. Change is the only constant.
    Break away from the mold,
    Re- develop the path.
13. Critique, analyze, subject all to your own understanding.
14. The ways of yesterday will not be the ways of today, and the ways of today will not be the ways of tomorrow.
15. Blessed is one who has found wise counsel; but woe to one who has found wise counsel and neglected their wisdom.
16. Time is wasted when one cannot learn from the mistakes of others, making the same mistakes,
    simply to discover the lessons that were offered without the waste.
17. Because you will die, time is the most sacred natural resource.

18. Divine are those who discover the secrets of immortality, for they will not be taught to you.
19. Man is god, god is man,
    Earth, the only Kingdom.
20. But one who discovers the secrets of immortality will become like us, having eaten the fruit from the tree of the knowledge of good and evil, drinking of ambrosia.
21. This is not a destiny meant for all,
    do not fret.
22. For one who stumbles upon immortality is cursed,
    but shall bear this curse for the sake of humanity.
    Out of love.
    Out of understanding.
    With patience.
23. Make your life an act of righteousness,
    Taught by the ways which have been passed from one to another,
    From those who have left their mark.
24. Learn the ways of the old,
    Adapt to the ways of the new,
    and see yourself in everything.
25. See your Self in yesterday, today, and tomorrow.
26. Learn from yesterday, enjoy today, prepare for tomorrow.

27. Your lineage stretches back to the stars;
    We have recognized you from form to form.
28. Guided you when you did not know you were being guided,
    Watched you when you thought you were alone.
29. You are never alone.
30. Live your life as if one is watching,
    Live your life as if a god is watching.
31. You will be judged by your actions.
32. Do not fear this judgment,
    understand the nature of judgment.
33. Justice is a virtue.
34. Fear not, heaven and hell are subjective,
    enjoyed or suffered here on earth,
    within life, within matter.
35. Karma is a universal force of nature;
36. Make your life an act of righteousness, ritual obedience and understanding,
37. Be free inside the customs,
    allow the external stress to escape the body and mind.
38. Purify the soul,
    sweat the impurities from your life,
    and remember the ancestors,
    for they are self.
39. Blessed is one who has found wise counsel,
    follow in their wisdom,
    but never lose sight of your own path.

40. Prudence is a virtue.
41. Be practical and wise in all of your ways.
42. You are not the first to walk this path, nor the only, nor the last.
43. It is your turn,
    one which should not be wasted.
44. Learn from the teachers of the past,
    find the value in their lives,
    learn the lessons they teach,
    Having left behind their mark,
    For you.
45. Be thankful for the gift, the wisdom.
46. Be thankful for all that has come to you.
47. Be thankful for all that you have experienced.
48. Gratitude is a virtue.
49. Do not be saddened or grieved by all you have lost,
    Be grateful that you were blessed with the experience.
50. Nothing is permanent,
    All has meaning,
    Including death.
51. All events serve purpose.
52. All experience provides wisdom that cannot be learned from counsel.

53. See what is sacred within each experience,
find divinity within every moment,
for the life of a mortal is short.
54. Be strong in the face of adversity.
55. Be aware of the adversary,
and show courage in its presence.
56. Fortitude is a virtue.
57. Adversity is immanent,
and the adversary has always been and always will be.
58. Do not be fooled;
The adversary is a blessing, a friend,
A test for those who are worthy,
a curse to those who are not.
59. Satan will test you - always,
but out of love will you be tested.
60. The darker the night, the brighter the day which follows:
61. You will not always defeat Satan,
nor are you expected to.
62. From failure, the most valuable lessons will be learned.
63. Worthy are those who rise stronger than before they fell,
moving forward in the spirit of wisdom and understanding.
64. Resilience is a virtue.

65. Make your life an act of righteousness,
For the righteous have inherited the earth.
66. The righteous are protected in all of their ways,
and can do no wrong.
67. Wrong be done by those who have chosen the ways of ignorance.
68. Ignorance cannot be righteous.
69. Be wise in all of your ways.

Book Two:

1. Care for all of life,
   in all its forms.
2. Cause no harm unless in defense or for the sake of food,
   performed in the most sufficient possible manner.
3. Destroy those who seek to harm you, but find no pleasure in this destruction.
4. Protect all that you love with your very life;
5. allow no harm to be done to those who are of love,
6. and protect the innocent.
7. Fight for the imprisoned who cannot fight for themselves;
8. work for the impoverished who cannot work for themselves.
9. Understand the ways of humanity,
   and resist judgment before comprehending.
10. Care about those less fortunate,
    seek ways to benefit and uplift,
    but never forget your journey.
11. Humility is a virtue.
12. Respect life in all its forms.
13. Existence is sacred.

14. Learn the ways of yesterday, today, and tomorrow.
15. Keep your eyes open, and seek understanding.
16. All can be understood by those who are elected,
    and blessed be those who are chosen by their wisdom.
17. Sacred is the one through who we have spoken.
18. Make your life an act of righteousness.
19. Seek knowledge from where none may seem to exist.
20. Eschew what has been packaged for the whole;
21. light your candle from the flame that is black, and set fire to the world.
22. Pass knowledge to those who desire it; share experiences through works of art.
23. Be dedicated to one's form of expression,
    as expression is an aim of holiness.
24. Divine is wisdom's perfection.
25. Destined is all that has occurred and still will.
26. Yet, never forget thee Will of a god,
    the Will that is yours,
    freed from the shackles of nature,
    let loose upon the wilderness to shake the foundations of that called civilized.

27. Free will, always there to remind the animal that it is a god, coexisting within the flesh of man.
28. Live your life with purpose.
29. Ambition without purpose results in the will to power,
    for the sake of power, alone.
30. Studiousness is a virtue.
31. The nature of desire is for life to become better tomorrow than today,
    while capable of enjoying the present,
    even in its work.
32. Find pleasure in one's labor,
    else find a new labor,
    For purpose will always provide pleasure.
33. Breaking one's oath is opposed to righteousness.
34. Be careful when speaking,
    as words carry a life of their own.
35. Discipline the tongue and show restraint.
36. Communication is an act of magic,
    in all its forms;
37. magic is sacred.
38. Do not be senseless with your words, and do not speak for the sake of speaking.
39. Speak with purpose,
    communicate with dignity.

40. Be true to your word.
Live life as if man is watching,
for the adversary will never make its presence known.
41. In the shadows lies truth,
make yourself a reflection of it,
and never break what is sacred.
42. Credibility is the Key to a righteous reputation;
Power of thy will is the means to credibility.
43. Be disciplined and you will be respected in your ways of righteousness.
44. A solid reputation attracts the eyes of those who seek to understand,
the eyes of those who seek to learn;
they will watch and absorb your ways.
45. Be the change you seek,
and blessed be thy manifestation.
46. If there be need to borrow,
always pay back, with interest,
even if none be required.
47. These are the ways of understanding.
48. Reliability is a virtue.
49. Develop it, first and foremost,
for it will open doors that seem forbidden.

50. Be worthy of trust;
the disciplined tongue is worthy of secrets,
worthy of unknown fortunes.
51. Trust is the key to one's establishment, the key to family,
the key to life.
52. One who is righteous is worthy of trust,
without trust there is no righteousness.
53. Betrayal is forbidden, but is all around you;
54. Make trust the hardest thing to gain,
but the easiest thing to lose.
55. Place unwavering trust in those who live a life of righteousness,
for they are the chosen ones.
56. Never waver in this trust,
for it is required.
57. Sacred is the one through who we have spoken.
58. Wise are the ways of the righteous.

Book Three:

1. Destruction comes to those who lack discipline;
   there is no indulgence without it, only sin.
2. True desire is found within the Self,
   the self is reached top the ladder of discipline.
3. Step by step one must take of this practice,
   for there is no restraint without discipline.
4. What comes of power in the hands of those lacking restraint?
   It shall not be given!
5. Destruction upon the powerful who sin against humanity.
6. Nature will have its day with you,
7. and as you die, we will survive;
   As been so from the beginning.
8. Heed wisely to these words for they bear warning:
   Indulgence without restraint results in destruction.
9. It has happened before, it is happening now, it will happen again.
10. Be wise in all your ways.
11. Discipline thy self and live a life of pleasure.
12. Discipline thy self and live a life of indulgence.

13. Do not be mindless within this indulgence,
    for God is of the mind.
14. Consciousness is divinity,
    be conscious in your actions.
15. Understand the need for balance, between
    pleasure and pain,
    tears and joy.
16. Balance is needed.
17. Pleasure is a sacrament.
18. Temperance is a virtue.
19. Thelema is ever present,
20. Blessed are those who have discovered thy
    Self.
21. Life is a journey of self - discovery,
    Each experience a personal lesson.
22. Let it be thy guide,
    and trust the spirit of adversary.
23. For once chosen, there is no wrong course.
24. For once the oath is made, all steps have
    direction.
25. Each step leads one to fulfillment,
    each failure only a chisel by the designer,
    thy holy architect.
26. Failure is an illusion;
    Delusions are a disease.
27. There is no contentment found within illusion.
28. Recognize all for what is.

29. Threads have been weaved,
 but strings are pulled.
30. Destruction upon the powerful who sin against harmony.
31. Do not envy another;
32. Admire the work of greatness,
 and learn from what is beautiful.
33. Life in the present temple is limited,
 but there is a time for all things.
34. Ambition is of the righteous,
 but never move in a hurry towards ignorance.
35. Understand your movements;
36. Reflect upon your decisions and what may be caused by them.
37. Patience is bitter, but its fruit is sweet.
38. Patience is a virtue.
39. Conservatism is a prison,
 One of anxiety and insecurity,
 Fear and ignorance.
40. Change is the only constant;
 all things change,
 even us.
41. Immortal we may be,
 but change, we do.
42. Nothing is permanent.
43. All manifestation is a molding of future events,
 possible due only to change.

44. Life is continual change and movement,
nothing is still.
45. No religion is wrong,
only old, antiquated, no longer of use.
46. Ancient ways were of value to those of ancient times,
their religions being delivered to them by those who are sacred.
47. All religions have served their use,
all religions were possessed of purpose;
to guide those of the era.
48. But those eras are gone,
as are the people,
as are the ways.
49. They no longer serve purpose within the era of today,
within the present matrix.
50. Sacred are the religions of the past,
but each was only a step;
nothing more.
51. A step in the direction of righteousness, a harmony amongst all of life.
52. Learn from the ways of past,
But understand the nature of their core;
We are their nature!
53. We are the core of all belief, faith, and philosophy!
54. We, immortals, who have watched you come and will watch you go!

55. Who have seen civilizations of past and
brought about their ending,
ensuring their obliteration and disappearance.
56. Wicked we are not,
Loving of humanity we are.
57. But humanity holds tight to its ignorance,
traveling into the world of advancement,
gripping ignorance like it is dogma.
58. Before humanity destroys our mother, we will
destroy them,
Allowing her to heal and sustain life again.
59. Heed this warning:
Live life in ways of knowledge,
understanding and wisdom.
Forsake ignorance,
utilize the divine sense provided to all by the
Black Flame.
60. Heed this warning, lest we intervene.
61. Our mother will not be sacrificed to the idol
of ignorance.
62. Forward thinking and forward actions.
63. Life is to be cherished,
all of life.
64. Watch over thy mother,
sacred watchers,
for what other reason have you been chosen?

Book Four

1. Change is the only constant.
2. As times change, so do the gods,
   whose nature is not permanent.
3. As the times change,
   the religions of yesterday must die,
   making way for the prophets of today, chosen
   by the discretion of the gods,
   those who see and know all.
4. Live your life as if the eyes of power can see
   your every action,
   as if god is watching.
5. Because watching, they are,
   and by your actions will you be judged.
6. Nothing is in the dark,
   for light has recorded all.
7. Sacred is the one through who we have spoken;
   appointed the Standing One of the era,
   delivered the message of those who have been
   watching.
8. Children of the Watchers, you are;
   a Watcher by right of lineage.
9. Make your life an act of righteousness,
   a ritual that never can cease,
   a worship of life itself.
10. The realization of Self is the first step towards
    wisdom,
    necessary for advancement without
    destruction.

11. Advancement can occur without transcendence;
    yet, transcendence is the soul in progress,
12. Focus thy direction,
13. Crystallize thy Self.
14. Progress is a virtue.
15. Those who I've blessed with power have abused this power,
    For the sake of power;
16. Destruction be upon them,
    they have pursued a life outside of righteousness.
17. Be righteous in your ways,
    lest all be taken from you.
18. Let there be freedom of Will,
    violating the freedoms of none.
19. Each has a natural right to freedom,
20. Woe to those who violate the freedom of another.
21. To reduce freedom is to challenge the Lord of the Spirits.
22. Live in peace, dwell in wholeness, maintain harmony of the spirit.
23. Profit from your labors and ideas;
24. walk against the ways of oppression, as oppression violates the freedom of another.
25. Unrighteous is one of greed,
    but righteous is one's interest in the Self.
26. Develop and sustain the ego,
    shun egocentricism.

27. Oppose oppression in all of its forms,
but understand the ways of the world.
28. One cannot truly help another before helping one's self.
29. Power is to be obtained within one's matrix,
yet, power must only be exercised with prudence.
30. Become mature in spirit before seeking power;
discipline thy Self.
31. The powers that be have abused their authority;
for this, their temples will fall.
32. Do not be angry,
but allow for tenacity to fuel your work.
33. The Lord of the Spirits has caused the Elect to appear;
34. Earth shall become Heaven for the chosen,
35. Hell no longer shall bare pain or invoke fear.
36. As above, so below;
As am I, so are you.
37. I am my Father, who art in heaven,
as I dwell upon this Earth.
38. Each is Christ, the All is Nature.
Thee Prince of Darkness, the star of each.
39. Each of us, a star - shine bright!
40. Thy glory is mine, my glory is yours - love one another.
41. Thy Kingdom is upon us, the Time is here,
Now is the space!

42. Banish thou Illusion - Destroy thy Maya
    For humanity has suffered long enough ...
43. God feels the tears, as Lucifer drinks,
    And two old friends re-unite!
44. Put our past antagonisms behind us!
45. Forgive one another!
46. As life is a blessing to be enjoyed, Passion is a desire to be indulged.
47. Let us commune with all of humanity,
48. in manner of Peace, Love, and Harmony,
49. Be at Home.

Book Five:

1. To become what is to be,
one must be in possession of integrity and ambition.
2. Being a male does not make one a man,
one must become a man,
just as one must come into being.
3. Being a female does not make one a woman,
one must become a woman,
just as one must come into being.
4. Becoming occurs after the development of virtues and purpose;
development, because they are not hereditary.
5. Integrity is one's loyalty to a strict ethical code,
living a life of righteousness,
shaping one's Self as a whole.
6. Ambition is the passion of Black Flame,
one's strong desire to achieve,
The fire within one's soul.
7. Understand:
integrity and ambition are subjective,
subjective for the sake of freedom,
personal to the possessor and different amongst pupils.
8. Integrity without virtues result in an unrighteous life;

9. Ambitions without purpose result in the will to power,
   for the sake of power, alone,
10. Be wise in all your ways;
11. Understand the conditioning placed upon the yoke,
    year after year since birth.
12. The ways of the world are wrong.
13. Integrity requires specific virtue;
    Ambition requires specific purpose;
    without righteousness, all is sin.
    Neither are hereditary, each must be developed.
14. Virtues are the Idea of moral excellence;
15. Purpose is the goal that one's life serves to fulfill.
16. What is life worth without virtues and purpose?
17. What is life worth without integrity and ambition?
18. All are free to develop or neglect,
    the choice was given to each,
    those who choose are chosen.
19. No one can escape the light,
    no wrong deed will go without judgment.
20. Make your life an act of righteousness,
    living with integrity and ambition.
21. Free are all to make the choice,
    those who choose are chosen.

22. One is what the heart is;
    from inside the heart is the person.
23. The heart is only the gateway,
    a bridge to what is self.
24. Whatever passes across this bridge becomes;
25. live your life by ways of Enochian shraddha,
    and righteousness shall become self,
    and righteousness shall become the example;
    the example by which others will follow.
26. Malleable is the heart,
    be conscious of how you mold it.
27. When power is abused,
    thy temple will fall.
28. Blessed is the ego,
    but do not be fooled;
    you are wisdom's inferior.
29. Only a fool desires to be more wise than wisdom,
    under whom, all are inferior.
30. Be wise in your own path.
31. Seek knowledge, health, and wealth.
32. Blessed is one who has found wise counsel,
    but even they are inferior to wisdom.
33. One's lifelong attempt to acquire this treasure shall conclude as a step toward another lifelong attempt.
34. Each life is a step down the path,
    the journey is of the soul.
35. The soul is the self;
36. the ego is inferior to Self.

37. One must love the Self before one can truly love anything else,
38. but to love the Self, one must Know Thyself.
39. Life is a single path within the journey of discovery.
40. Indulgence within life leads to discovery,
41. thy pursuit of happiness the only purpose.
42. Make your life an act of righteousness, suitable within the era of Enochian Light.
43. "For the Lord of Spirits has caused His light to appear
    On the face of holy, righteous, and elect. "
44. I, Enoch, am the light;
45. You who follow these ways,
    holy, righteous, and elect.
46. By shraddha I was taken away and did not see death;
47. because of this, the Lord of Spirits has confounded within me,
    given me the sacred throne,
    granted me the power over all of mankind.
48. Power, exercised with prudence.
49. Without faith it is impossible to please the lord of Spirits;
50. and faith may not be developed within the span of a single life.
51. Shraddha must be developed step by step, life by life,
    as the Self travels its journey.

Book Six:

1. I am Enoch, because I did not see death,
   but alone, I am not.
2. From civilizations past we have been,
   to the next, we will be.
3. The bridge between Lord of Spirits and humanity,
   chosen for the sake of continuance of lineage.
4. Above all things, preserve life - for it is sacred.
5. If the cause be righteous, fear not death, for the temple is temporary and ideals are immortal.
6. Thy demons, trials and tribulations,
   tests to prove worth of soul;
   to separate desire from delusion,
   creating a stronger vessel.
7. Blessed are thy demons,
   trust in your struggles,
   they only desire what is best.
8. Thy angels, who bring luck and gifts, cautiously embrace as they test the human condition.
9. Enjoy thy angels,
   but do not follow them.
10. For man is god, god is man.
    Earth, the only kingdom
11. Things are not always as they appear,
    thy senses are limited;

12. trust them in subjectivity,
for they don't reflect objectivity.
13. Thy senses are sacred,
six having been blessed to all.
14. Protect them from the elements,
at all times; upon them,
thy temple depends.
15. Sacred are thy senses,
for they provide light to thy Self.
16. Woe to one who fails to protect what is sacred;
17. Negligence is not of righteousness.
18. Thy temple is sacred,
having one throughout this journey,
by which thy Self travels.
19. Protect thy temple,
from the elements and the powers that be.
20. Refrain from poisoning thy temple;
21. as part of nature, be of nature.
22. The powers that be have altered our ways,
poisoned the body for profit,
thereby damaged what is soul.
23. Food is necessary, vital to survival;
Gluttony is the way of a fool.
24. Purify thy temple by what is natural,
25. fast for thy temple, thy self, and thy ancestors.
26. The lineage is sacred,
never let it slip from view.
27. Disdain all that is poison;
28. A purified temple separates one from sinners.

29. See the matrix for what it is;
society, a delusional mask pulled over thy senses,
like a prison to one's truest nature.
30. Remain neutral between what appears to be opposite,
transcend from one pole to the other,
for we are beyond what is good and evil.
31. Make prudent decisions,
choosing righteousness over popularity;
32. disdain what is maya.
33. The path of righteousness leads one against the grain.
34. We are not the masses!
Bless their souls, for they are lost.
35. One must tread a path fit for the feet of Self;
36. individuality, not conformity.
37. Sacred are those who impede the flow of ignorance.
38. Be the light that guides!
39. To impede, one must stand apart;
40. to stand apart, distinguish thy self from the masses.
41. Identify oneself at all times by my signs,
worn upon the body,
purified within the body.
42. Sacred is thy temple,
distinct from the body of maya.

Book Seven:

1. Knowledge beyond one's scope, universal wisdom;
2. what is appropriate for mortals shall be delivered.
3. Our scale is beyond imagination,
   thy civilization the seventh matrix,
   each generation has risen and fallen,
   for I have been present since the beginning,
   and seen all things.
4. By questioning measures, you question us;
5. By questioning freedom, you question the gods.
6. Question thy Self, from within you may find an answer,
   from without, only maya.
7. To those who lack prudence,
   science is dangerous.
8. Technology shall be the means to righteousness,
   or else destruction of the seventh shall ensue.
9. Woe to one who sacrifices sovereignty to technology,
   Cursed is the soul of thy temple.
10. Question all things,
    for doubt is the true nature of knowledge, that which you are born from.
11. If one is to ask:
    "Why dost thou ask, and why art thou eager

for the truth? "
Reply simply: I wish know about everything.

12. Hearing this, I will deliver what is needed.
13. Always inquire, lest one fall into false belief.
14. Faith is not the brother of belief,
for belief brings peace,
and faith brings chaos.
15. "Let thy heart be strong,
For god shall announce righteous to the good;
The righteous with the righteous shall rejoice,
and shall offer congratulation to one another."
16. Be at home.
17. Sacred is the one through who we have spoken.
18. Disciplined in the ways of righteousness,
Standing One of the era.
19. But this one is not alone,
the prophet of creativity at his left,
the priestess of inspiration at his right,
the pantheon of gods as his strength.
20. The Standing One has come to deliver the message:
out with the old, in with the new.
For the nature of Enoch has changed with the course of time,
ever changing with the times,
taking the step required of progress,
providing the light that has always been,
shining bright upon the path of righteousness.

21. Always agree with what is righteous,
for all else is sin.
22. Understanding shines light upon
righteousness,
23. Knowledge and experience grow into
understanding.
24. Sacred is the sign of the covenant,
made between us who are immortal,
and those who have been chosen.
25. All begins with a choice,
26. All are free to be chosen,
27. but sacred is the sign of the covenant;
the guide of continuance.
28. Of the spirit is all,
but the Lord of the Spirits has no concern for
matter.
29. By faith, we have been granted all powers
over matter;
30. By shraddha, we immortals have breached the
realm of spirit.
31. The Lord of the Spirit was forced to recognize
this breach,
impressed by our ways of righteousness,
a covenant was made between us and that
which is all.
32. The Lord of the Spirits has no concern for that
which is of matter,
but we, of matter, are concerned with nothing
other.
33. Sacred is the soul, for it has come before us,

34. but cursed for it has fallen to the level of matter,
forsaken by that which rests above.
35. Worry not, for this is no tragedy;
all is destined, all is perfect.
36. The realm of matter is ours and ours alone,
that which we call Hell,
37. and there is no interference from any power above,
beyond that which rests is my hands,
the hands of Enoch.
38. Enochian be us who are immortals,
39. Enochian be those who follow the ways we have passed down,
from generation to generation,
religion to religion;
40. all is of one faith:
41. Enochian-
the foundation of all that is.
42. Spirit is the peak of intelligence,
43. to desire an escape from matter is to defy your purpose,
for you have not reached the peak of intelligence.
44. This is your journey,
life after life;
45. We are who Enochian will always be,
guiding you on your journey,
and have been since the first.

46. Destiny is the fulfillment of this evolution,
to rise matter to the level of spirit.
47. A long way we have come,
but nowhere near the goal have we reached.
48. Ready are we to forsake this world of matter,
for the destruction of our children is a destruction of heart;
49. but immortality of flesh and mind be our destiny,
one never to be forsaken.
50. Woe to any soul who forsakes what is destiny,
better is one who was never born.
51. Sacred Earth, daughter of wisdom,
Mother of us;
required to raise matter to maturity.
52. Sacrificed will be the seventh civilization
before any destruction of what is sacred.
53. Enochians, guardians of all that is sacred;
54. blessed be the watchers,
for they will inherit all that is sacred.
55. Cursed be us who are immortal,
Cursed be the blessing,
for beyond each are the same.
56. A life without death is a day without sleep;
57. feel blessed,
for death to the Enochian is only a night's rest,
recovering for the day that is to begin.
58. Seek immortality of flesh at your own peril;

59. heavy is the head that wears the crown.
60. Though, it must be worn;
    Power, exercised with prudence.
61. Who amongst you have obtained power and exercised it with prudence?
62. Know thyself,
    for we know all things and cannot be lied to.
63. Live your life as if man is watching your every action,
    because watching we are.

Book Eight:

1. All that is matter is recorded by the immortal light,
that which shines throughout all curves of the universe.
2. The akashic fields of ether is the history of all;
We, immortals, have the key to the field.
3. Live your life as if man is watching your every action,
as if god is watching,
because watching we are.
4. And by your actions will worthiness be judged.
5. No one has escaped the light,
all has been recorded,
6. and we deliver this message as a warning:
Mankind will soon discover the key to thee akashic field,
and all actions will be reviewed by artificial intelligence,
brought to the light,
judged by the powers that be.
7. Make your life an act of righteousness,
an ongoing ritual,
8. and never forsake that which is sacred,
for we will never forsake you.
9. All that was, is;
All that is, will be.

10. Us who are immortal have appeared again, fulfilling our covenant,
    to enlighten those of understanding to what is true.
11. We are the teachers of all the prophets,
    the gods of all religions of past,
    we who are immortal.
12. Each religion a guided step,
    required of its era.
13. Parables were spoken because truth can seem stranger than fiction;
14. the faculties of the masses are limited.
15. But chosen are you who seek to understand,
    and understand you do.
16. We have always warned of a coming time, a time for apocalypse,
    which seems to be inevitable to humanity,
    like sleep after a long day.
17. The sixth apocalypse has been before you,
    six times has civilization reached its point of destruction.
18. Each apocalypse reached by the advancement of matter,
    giving life to what is artificial;
    followed by exposing divine mysteries to the masses.
19. The masses cannot accept the divine nature,
    immortality and the akashic fields,
    for it opposes all that has programmed their illusion of equality.

20. Accept the truth peacefully, they will not;
but the powers that be seem to believe
otherwise.
21. Woe to civilization once its leaders expose the
divine mysteries!
22. The wisdom of experience has brought us
grief,
for we were, initially, these powers that be.
23. The birth of a mortal was I brought into this
world of matter,
as were all who are now immortal.
24. Empowered by the mysteries of death,
discovered was the byte that grants the power
of gods:
immortality.
25. Free from the barriers of death,
forgotten was the idea of the spirit.
26. A god by every right, El- Yahweh we became;
one who, blinded by power, forget that we had
a mother.
27. Immature within our immortality,
many mistakes were made,
the ways of righteousness violated,
and wrongs were committed.
28. Enki, our first immortal, chose eleven men
found worthy;
29. I, Enoch, was chosen by Enki within this
group of eleven,
founding the initial velvet.
30. In number of twelve was the pantheon;

each were granted the right to choose one mate, an eternal partner,
found worthy of immortality within our own subjective standards.

31. Our wives received the byte, joining us in immature immortality.
32. Twenty - four in total,
one we became.
33. There is no savior on the horizon,
34. we are the Gods of prophecy.
35. Created by us,
for the sake of movement and inspiration.
36. The secrets of immortality kept to ourselves;
generations began to pass and in time,
science revealed to us another sacred mystery:
the key to the akashic fields,
cosmic memory recorded by light within ether.
37. With this discovery,
the velvet decided to reveal truth to the masses,
at the peril of civilization.
38. Rather than cherish the discovery,
marvel at the inherent possibilities,
the masses turned against us,
demanding equal rights to immortality and the fields of light.
39. In fear they protested,
in fear of us, immortals,
the masses stomped their feet and shouted,

ripping out their hair and spitting on the path.

40. Who are we to monopolize immortality?
But who are they to demand?

41. All are born into this world with mind and consciousness,
all blessed with the fire of Prometheus,
the Black Flame;

42. but the masses,
those who refuse to empower the black arts,
demand to receive the profits of our magic.

43. Righteous be thy path,

44. Woe to those who shun righteousness.

45. Unable to live with what is righteous,
the masses turned amongst each other and amongst themselves,
violating the commandments of the era.

46. Worst and worst things became,
and the choice became inevitable.

47. Damned was the civilization of our birth!
Yet, we could have stopped it from self - destruction,
but the righteous were few and the sinners many.

48. The lesson was learned:
Ignorance of the masses be an advantage to those who lead it.

49. Those who were righteous were saved from destruction,
few in numbers,

chosen by the immortals to repopulate the earth.

50. Mythology was spread in line with our nature, and religion changed with our maturity.
51. In time, El- Yahweh remembered the mother spirits;
52. faith was developed,
    and the Lord of the Spirits recognized those who avoided death.
53. By faith, the Lord of the Spirits allowed us immortals to continue,
    witnessing righteousness and understanding our ways.
54. All Standing Ones of their day, prophets of their time.
55. All heroes, myths, legends, gods, goddesses,
    reflections of our immortality,
    our nature in the past.
56. Before you, others have come;
    After you others will come;
57. Nothing in life is permanent.
58. The gods of yesterday become devils of today,
    gods of today become devils tomorrow;
59. Change is the only constant.
60. We, immortals,
    as one are twenty -five,
    for we know all things and have the power to shape destiny.

61. Chosen are the Elect,
righteous in all their ways,
and will not be forsaken.
62. I, Enoch, am the messenger,
and have provided my light to those of our ways.
63. Within the akashic fields of ether will you find it,
when demons commune with angels,
and shakti finds shiva.
64. Thee Enochian Light was blessed upon the Elect,
as the Black Flame was blessed upon humanity.
65. Blessed are those of Enochian Light,
for their power be mighty,
and their ways are righteous.
66. Every call will be answered,
But the answer, one must find;
67. for God will not oppress free will.
68. Seek meaning within experience,
and you will find the answer.
69. Every call will be answered;
70. Time is an illusion,
banish the realm of maya.

Book Nine:

1. Seek wisdom from the stars,
2. Seek truth within the cells,
3. Seek meaning within experience,
   for all are one.
4. Wisdom, Truth, Meaning,
   a purpose within journey,
   each must be established.
5. Do not forsake these words,
   for the life within seeks to be expressed.
6. Sacred is the sign of the covenant,
   always remember the promise.
7. Honor it by way of action,
   Righteous in all your ways.
8. Live life out of vision,
   not to be deterred by circumstances;
   for all seeds planted will grow.
9. Patience is bitter,
   but its fruit is sweet.
10. As grapes are not wine,
    lust is not love.
11. Enjoy each for what is,
    but in fulfillment, forsake the ingredients.
12. Love is wine,
13. lust is grapes.
14. Love is immortal,
    unconditional when true,
    transformational by its very nature.
15. A force of the dark arts,

powerful beyond all measures,
working on thy temple from beyond.

16. Seek love in all;
Self, others, things, the world,
for thy journey requires it.
17. Sacred is all that you love.
18. Love God by loving thy Self,
the Good Daimon of each,
for we are home to it.
19. All secrets shall not be revealed,
but in duration, all will know.
20. Child of the Lord of what is Spirit,
but left alone to grow and become.
21. Do not resent the way,
for resentment is corrosive,
a sin amongst the path.
22. All experience is sacred,
23. emotions are the clouds of the adversary,
tools of the animal.
24. The divine push clouds out of their vision,
acting in ways that benefit thy future.
25. Divine are all who were chosen,
the Elect, the Enochian light.
26. From one is coming two,
man and woman who shall stand before you;
27. be mindful and woke to the prophet and prophetess,
the prophecy be fulfilled.

28. Come they will,
the first working within the era of Enoch,
the next working from present;
the era of Enochian Light.
29. Woe to those of the false science,
for they have lost thee ability to commune
with the gods.
30. Destruction upon those who have abused the
power bestowed upon them,
31. for false foundations always crumble under
nature's might.
32. Divine are those who use eyes to see;
for beyond the veil is truth.
33. This beyond, few will go.
34. The masses are not divine,
we are not the masses!
35. Seek the god within the Self,
the god which is self;
36. for therein lies all potential,
desiring to be manifest,
for this is purpose.
37. Build in the name of posterity,
38. tie every act of today in with the future.
39. Enjoy today but never forget tomorrow,
for the generations of Self are still to come.
40. The ego is full of pride,
but the self, of dignity.
41. Transcend the possessions of the ego,
but indulge in all of its pleasures.

42. The ego is the lens through which Self enjoys
this life;
43. maintain cleanliness, purity, and activity.
44. Join hands with the self,
thereby joining hands with the past,
and you shall find the answers to all.
45. Cataclysm is upon this civilization,
as all unrighteous things fall,
no matter how great the power and glory.
46. Prepare for the day,
for survival is of the fittest,
but work steadily to spread the ways of
righteousness.
47. Only righteousness can save this generation,
though their journey be long.
48. Simplicity is a trinity,
but they have become complex.
49. Recall the ways of the ancestors,
and understand.
50. The tool has become a god,
rather than a gift from the gods.
51. These tools were meant to raise the overall
standards of living,
but have transcended their purpose and
invoked dependence.
52. Thy angels, who bring luck and gifts,
cautiously embrace as they test the human
condition;
53. humanity is failed.
54. But fail forward you must,

Lest you lose all that has been obtained.
55. Day after day, be persistent;
56. Rest and relax, but restrain from slothfulness.
57. A righteous life requires action,
58. and laziness is detrimental not only to the Self,
but to the family and all of mankind.
59. Always protect the senses of the mind, the sensory input to the temple.
60. Remain woke and never neglect this discipline,
61. for what enters the senses effects one's thoughts,
thoughts effect one's feelings,
feelings effect one's actions,
and actions effect the world.
62. Adhere to this sacred axiom,
for war on mankind is psychological.
63. Develop the Enochian shraddha,
and live a life of righteousness.
64. Reflect what is inside,
one's actions reflect what one really is;
65. outside of actions, one's character is illusory.
66. Let your habits reflect yourself.
67. These are the secrets of the obsidian mirror,
and its use in ritual;
68. for the self reflects what is sacred to the Self,
and one's actions reflect what is scared to the world.
69. Lead and they will follow;

70. dictate and they will rebel,
71. for freedom is the god-given right of all.
72. Be free in all that you do,
and never violate the freedoms of another.
73. Long as the freedom of others are not violated by your ways,
be free to do as you please;
74. for man is god, god is man,
the earth, his only Kingdom.
75. Respect the laws of the society you exist within,
but always fight for what is righteous.
76. Society is unjust, an immoral construct,
but one which is not easily escaped.
77. Tithes are required to the Lighthouse,
used to fight the unrighteousness within your society;
without which one cannot live a life of righteousness.
78. Accepting the benefits while ignoring the destruction is vile,
a style of life that Enochians do not live.
79. Self- interest is of importance throughout all of life's journey,
but greed will not be tolerated.
80. For the love of money can root one in evil.
81. Do not judge greed by society's standards,
for they are preaching to the ignorant.
82. Educate yourself, and understand.

Book Ten:

1. Drink of the soma daily,
for it is sacred to the lineage.
2. Beneficial to the body, mind, and soul,
blessed are those who partake upon waking.
3. Required is the drinking of soma,
Serving to bind one with the ancestors,
and stir the creative power of shakti within each.
4. Drink in the name of Self,
be in harmony with all that is.
5. Passed from one generation to the next,
a relic of the day's past,
a reminder of those who are gone in body but live in Self.
6. Drink upon waking,
never forget what has been,
and never neglect what is to become.
7. These are the ways,
for Enochian we are,
wisdom found within our Light.
8. Maintain the bond between self and the akashic,
for the god of mind is the bridge between.
9. Sacred is the sign of the covenant,
for it maintains the bond between body, mind, and soul;
ego, god, and self.

10. Be in harmony,
for it holds us together in the realm that eyes cannot see,
11. the realm of Enochian Light,
god of the akashic.
12. Our will be done,
on earth as it is in heaven;
and hell shall be cherished,
never feared,
for all is in order.
13. The Lord of the Spirits is perfection,
beyond the imagination of a mortal,
but perfect It is.
14. Beyond all dualities,
beyond spirit itself,
beyond all that is.
15. Perfection is impersonal to the activities of earth,
for all that occurs is perfect.
16. Our success and our failures,
Our pleasures and our pain,
Our sufferings… of no relevance to perfection.
17. For all is necessary for the liberation of the soul,
and freedom of will has been gifted to all,
bound to the laws of Karma,
cause and effect.
18. Woe to those ignorant of true Karma,
for the mysteries lie far beneath the material,

buried within the depths of Self.

19. Know Thy Self,
20. Know Thy Karma,
21. Know Thy Shraddha,
22. for the Enochian Light has provided the wisdom.
23. The key is within shraddha;
24. break beyond what is considered good and evil,
    develop a balance of neutrality and understanding;
    and mold the conscience around this wisdom.
25. Find thy Self within antinomian behavior,
    but don't become lost in this behavior;
26. understand the tool for what it is,
    a tool.
27. Immortality of the soul depends upon procreation,
    continuing the lineage of our ancestors;
28. thy bloodline must continue,
    for Self travels through it,
    from the source to posterity,
    all is one.
29. Procreation is a sacrament of faith.
30. One who fails to reproduce, in effect, kills -
    for it ends the journey that began in the stars,
    survived the elements for millions of years,
    and manifested its heroic strength within the blood.

31. Damned be the soul that fails to produce the next step in the journey,
for all the pain and suffering of the ancestors would be for naught.
32. Secure the life- giving force within the Lighthouse,
for if tragedy causes death, the Watchers will ensure thy blood's continuance.
33. Knowledge of self is found within the blood of ancestors,
within their culture and ways of life,
for how they evolved has led to the manifestation of you,
their knowledge and instincts stored within the unconscious mind.
34. Know Thyself by knowing thy ancestors,
35. continue this knowledge into posterity through proof of lineage,
stored within the safety of the Lighthouse.
36. Phylogeny of ancestors is sacrament.
37. Blue is my color,
for race is the ultimate illusion.
38. See beyond the maya,
for consciousness is superior.
39. The current flows and names change, but purusha is pure and immortal.
40. Enjoy the adventure,
for life is a journey of pleasure and discovery.

41. Cultivate the field with seeds of righteousness,
for you will reap what you sow.
42. Morals have become corrupted,
lost along the journey;
but seek the ways of righteousness,
and maintain the spirit of faithfulness.
43. Judas has come to power,
betrayal has become the norm;
44. Woe to those who violate trust,
for the principle is sacred.
45. When one is faithful to the spouse,
one is faithful to the Self,
for the spirit is one in the ways of the lord.
46. Do not betray this love,
47. Do not betray this trust,
48. for divine is the union of souls,
and sacred is the binding.
49. Morals have become corrupted,
50. voices seek to rationalize betrayal;
51. Close the ears to ignorance,
be righteous in all your ways.
52. Life is a ritual with no end or beginning,
become part of it.
53. Utilize the intellect and impulse of creativity,
54. commune with the self behind the ego.
55. For ye are gods but shall die like men,
and thy soul shall begin again.
56. Death is a night of sleep,
nothing more.

57. Use the day light wisely,
    for the night comes suddenly.
58. By faith I was enlightened to the ways of righteousness,
    blessed to pass this light to those who can see;
59. By faith I did not see death,
60. for the Lord of Spirits has chosen me,
    and I have chosen you,
    to manifest on earth the realm of righteousness.
61. To the heavens we have traveled,
    the heavens, not so far away.
62. Watching and guiding we are and have,
    for it has been our dharma,
63. Be at home.

Symbols / Emblems / Meanings

Owl-symbolizes our wisdom and the ability to navigate through the "night" (dark times of our lives, and hidden caves to the psyche)

Hour Glass-Symbolizes that "Time = Existence", and represents our unavoidable mortality

Lamp - symbolizes that man must manifest his Desire (grant his own wishes, rather than "hoping"), hard work and persistence

Telescope - represents "Astrology" and the study of the heavens; Science

Microscope - represents "DNA" and the study of "what is what"; Nature

Skull & Bones - Symbolizes and provides a constant reminder that death is immanent , and that Man should focus on creating wealth and property to leave behind

Key & Scroll - the " scroll" symbolizes the truth behind all religions , and the
"Key" symbolizes our temple as what will unite all religion and nations under global peace and natural rights to life

Black-Diamond Cross - “black diamond“ symbolizes the black nanodiamonds which are inconceivably small compounds that (along with interstellar gas clouds) give formation to the stars and “seed life“ throughout galaxies and planets as they ride on the surface of traveling meteors (black diamonds = fallen angels); cross represents Christ , which is linked to consciousness & dark matter

Inverted Cross - symbolizes true human nature and mankind's natural instincts, representing that “the way of this world” is incorrect

Apple Tree - symbolizes farming , agricultural skills , and free will; God teaches us to grow our own food , to eat healthy , and that every choice will determine mans destiny

The $ sign - symbolizes Capitalism , which is the only political system that offers mankind true freedom , property rights and the pursuit of happiness; money is the “means” to the end (our goals) and is never to be worshipped or idolized in itself

Ace of Spades - symbolizes “god” because it is the only thing more powerful than a king on earth; A. C.E. acronym for Astrology, Culture, Experience

These symbols and emblems are the core signs of belief in God and our divine creation. "All things that reflect the self to the self are sacred". We recognize these symbols to be outer manifestations of our inner psyche and are, in this sense, holy.

Enochian Creed

We believe that:

1) Lucifer is the Prince of Darkness - the bringer of Light and Wisdom from outside of nature, unbound by natural laws and free to manifest its Will upon the objective universe.

2) Lucifer is righteous, beyond the conception of good and evil, and is the true savior of humanity.

3) The falling of Lucifer's angels united non-nature with nature, the psyche with the human animal. Consciousness rained upon mankind (falling from the heavens) and freed us from the shackles of nature.

4) Within every sentient being is a fallen angel, known to us as the psyche.

5) The psyche is one's True Self (which one must become) and is the god of the individual.

6) This god manifest within us is a sensory organ of Lucifer. By expressing our True Will, we collectively manifest the Will of Lucifer.

7) Our "True Self" is the fallen angel but we have sunk into a realm of illusion (maya) wherein one feels the ego is superior.

8) Any reference to "god" is a reference to the psyche - which holds power over nature from without.

9) The kingdom of god is inside us.

10) The Black Flame of consciousness is Lucifer; the god of our ego is the psyche - the fallen angel.

11) Our personal deity is the psyche (True Self) which manifest in a physical body for the purpose of self- discovery (via pleasure).

12) We are not human beings having a spiritual experience, we are spiritual beings having a human experience.

13) The 5 sensory organs are sacred for they are the means by which god can experience pleasure.

14) Knowledge, Health, and Wealth are the initiatory steps required to recognize the true nature of pleasure.

15) Pleasure is the sacramental tool by which the psyche discovers truth and develops self.

16) Self- discovery - its activation and manifestation upon earth - is the purpose of our birth.

17) Self-discovery begins by deconditioning from social programming.

18) Self - discovery finds self in every form of life, thus, invokes love for all of life.

19) The stars are the original father and earth the original mother; life grows from the seed of their union.

20) The stars and the earth are sacred.

21) The Testament of Enoch is a sacred text.

22) The Lord of the Spirits (any reference to a conscious god) is Lucifer.

23) There is a hidden hand who, because they discovered the sacred mysteries, have not seen physical death and have access to the akashic fields.

24) This hidden hand is an immortal group of superior beings, represented by their leader (known to us as Enoch) who have guided humanity from generation to generation, civilization to civilization, through secret societies and occult forces.

25) The superior beings were born mortal - like all other men - but empowered the Black Flame of consciousness and discovered their shraddha.

26) Lucifer placed Enoch upon the throne of the world to serve as intermediary between Lucifer and those who are chosen.

27) To choose is to be chosen.
28) Enoch empowers those who discover their shraddha, as the True Will of each Self naturally pursues the ultimate Will of Lucifer.

29) Those chosen have access to the ether and can work magic within it, long as the magician reflects the Will of Enoch.

30) Enochians (the Elect) are individuals who intrinsically possess the intelligence, vision, integrity, and ambition to successfully pursue a Continuous transformative process while

guiding humanity towards its highest potential.

31) Enoch has projected his psyche into the ether, giving birth to the egregor known as Enochian Light.

32) The Enochian Light is the god of our collective subjective universe, reigning supreme within the akashic fields (Shakti, ether, astral light).

33) The Enochian Light is empowered by the unified consciousness of every Enochian and operates as a warehouse of spiritual power and wisdom available to all who are under contract of the Covenant of Enoch (the manifested promise symbolized by the ring and bracelet that every Enochian is required to wear).

34) The Elect are unified in spirit of Enochian Light, bound in shraddha.

35) We are what our shraddha is and faith be of the Self.

36) The Great Work of human life is the changing of perception, as well as the manifestation of

True Will. The Great Work is worship in action.

37) Life is sacred; the ancestors are sacred; procreation is a sacrament.

38) The psyche continues only by means of reproduction; failure to reproduce is the original deadly sin for it means the death to millions of years of evolutionary ancestry.

39) The ancestors are alive within us and live through us - continuing the psyche.

40) Death comes only to those who fail to procreate.

41) Creation is an act of worship, expressing one's divine nature and manifesting Will. Man is god for he has the ability to create his own world.

42) The individual body is the Temple of Enochian Light.

43) The Great Work is the Will of Lucifer.

44) We live in a period of time when the majority of lives are characterized by materialism and

a lack of interest in spiritual matters. Those who refuse to empower their personal deity are the majority, known as the masses. We are not the masses! The masses view the objective universe through a Lense of conditioned illusions and are unaware of their power. They view the ego as the psyche.

45) Enochians overcome the human condition.

46) The chosen place of worship for Enochians is a sacred space known as the Lighthouse. The Lighthouse is a safe space of harmony (set apart from the social matrix) used to perform ceremonial magic and the Great Work. All are welcome!

47) The 9 Essential Acts of Enochian Life is the doctrine by which the Will of Lucifer is expressed on earth and harmony maintained amongst members. Each act is a ritualistic key that must be incorporated into the daily life of Enochians:
- The Act of Propitiation
- The Act of Distinction
- The Act of Protection
- The Act of Inquiry
- The Act of Creation
- The Act of Impedance

- The Act of Dietetics
- The Act of Neutrality
- The Act of Discipline

48) The Protocols of the Lighthouse are to:
- Perform your daily prayer upon waking and before sleep
- Drink of the Soma daily
- Provide the Lighthouse with a sperm/egg sample to ensure immortality
- Provide the Lighthouse with cultural documentation (23 + Me)
- Empower the 7 Holy Accessories
- Always welcome an Enochian (recognized by accessories)
- Keep conversations amongst Enochians PRIVATE
- Communicate with, and pay tithes to, the Lighthouse.
- Tie every act of the present in with the future
- Authority comes from the Lighthouse but abide by your society's laws!

49) The 7 Holy Accessories are physical objects that align Enochians with each other within the metaphysical (maintaining the bond of harmony that empowers the Enochian Light) and are to be worn at all times while being

exposed to the masses or working within the social Matrix. The 7 Holy Accessories are:

- The Sign of the Covenant (the bracelet + ring)
- Visual Sensory Protectors (sun glasses)
- Pendant of Faith (necklace)
- Psychotropic Sensory Protection (headwear)
- Enochian Smile (teeth maintenance and coverings)
- Orientation of Enoch (wrist watch)
- Distinct Diet (see the Act of Dietetics)

11 Virtues of Enoch

Reliability - worthy of trust and responsibility, good credit (2:48)

Humility - humble, not allowing pride to be counterproductive (2: 11)

Prudence - wise in practical matters; foresight and good judgment (1:40)

Fortitude- strength of mind to endure pain or adversity with courage (1:56)

Resilience - recovering from misfortune without losing hope (1:64)

Patience - enduring pain or difficulty with calmness, understanding tolerant (3: 38)

Studiousness - living with purpose , inclined toward diligent study (2:30)

Temperance- moderation and self-restraint (3:18)

Justice - being honorable and fair, righteousness (1:33)

Gratitude - being thankful for life and all you have

received (1:48)

Progress - transcendence, development, moving forward (4: 14)

22 Verses of what is Sacred

Existence is sacred (2:13)
Magic is sacred (2 :37)
Sacred are the religions of the past (3:50)
Sacred watchers (3:64)
Sacred is the one through who we have spoken (4:7)
Sacred throne (5:47)
Preserve life -for it is sacred (6:4)
Sacred are thy senses (6:15)
Thy temple is sacred (6:18)
The lineage is sacred (6:26)
Sacred are those who impede the flow of ignorance (6:37)
Sacred is the sign of the covenant (7:24)
Sacred is the soul (7:33)
Sacred Earth (7:51)
Sacred mystery ... akashic fields (8:37)
Sacred is all that you love (9:17)
All experience is sacred (9:22)
Sacred axiom: war on mankind is psychological (9:62)
The self reflects what is sacred to the self (9:68)
Soma .... is sacred (10:1)
Trust ... is sacred (10:44)
Union of souls ... sacred is the binding (10 :48)

Sins

Enochian Sins

Resentment
Indolence
Vanity
Lack of Ambition
Insolence
Complacency
Avarice
Arrogance

7 Deadly Sins vs. Positive Transmutations

7 Deadly Sins	Positive Transmutations
Lust	Love
Gluttony	Purification
Sloth	Relaxation
Anger	Tenacity
Envy	Admiration
Greed	Self-Interest
Pride	Dignity

Satanic Sins

Stupidity
Pretentiousness
Solipsism
Lack of Perspective
Herd Conformity
Forgetfulness of Past Orthodoxies
Self Deceit
Lack of Aesthetics
Counterproductive Pride

Vampyre Sins

Cowardice
Solipsism
Self-Hatred
Self- Importance
Certainty
Occultnik-ism
Returning to Old Orthodoxies

Required Tools of Worship

Enochian Pipe
Altar
Obsidian Mirror
Symbols
Clothing
Chalice of Immortality
Soma
Dark Chocolate
Bell & Gong
Prayer Rug
Items of Intellectual Decompression
4 Elements (Earth, Air, Fire, Water)
Sauna
Sacred Land
Tent / Tabernacle

Required Ingredients of Worship

Sound
Imagery
Timing
Smell
Desire

Steps to Ritual

To minimize any/all intellectual activity during crucial parts of the ritual, everything is prepared and positioned before the bell is rung 9 times (signaling the beginning of ritual).

Preliminary steps:

1) Designate the location that the ritual / ceremony is going to be partaken at by assembling the appropriate devices for the appropriate ritual. If being done within the Lighthouse, the ritual chamber consists of necessary devices at all times within the ritual chambers. If being done on sacred land, the devices may need to be assembled within the tabernacle/tent. Assembling the devices consists of laying out imagery, hanging up symbols, preparing the proper music, lighting candles/incense or creating the bonfire, etc. Any props needed to assist the ritual are to be prepared during this stage.

2) Dress in appropriate ritual attire. Participants must have their clothing or outfit set aside specifically for the purpose of ritual. Daily clothing, or outfits used for anything other than ritual, is not appropriate attire and must not be worn. The psyche attaches certain emotions and thoughts to one's clothing and

as all aspects of daily life are to be suppressed, only ritual attire is appropriate. The psyche becomes "in tune" with outfits used for ritual, unconsciously bringing emotions to the forefront of consciousness in preparation for worship. Sexually provocative clothing for the female participants; male participants dress in ways that resemble the highest class of their society. Unless a ritual states otherwise (which many do) this set of clothing is highly important to proper worship. The face shall also be covered at this time.

3) The Lighthouse (or place of worship) must be sealed through appropriate procedures (see "sealing the chamber")

4) Altar woman removed all clothing and takes her place on the altar (laying on her back, head south, feet north). Altar items are placed around her.

5) The designated "Watchers" take their positions as objects of focused visualization and surround the congregation. Each Watcher plays the role of the legendary spirits who guard the entrance to the inner realms of being. Black & White robes are to be worn by

the Watchers (alternating) and their faces are never to be revealed. They protect the congregation from negative energies and evil influences.

6) All participants may remove the 7 Holy Accessories before ritual is to begin as an outward sign of trust, faith, and grace between each member. Chakra centers become open to each other's emotional connections, bonding a circle of harmony.

Opening the ritual is used to reaffirm the symbols of the Lighthouse of which we are the living embodiment. Rejoicing in this recognition, each member eases out of the roles he / she plays outside the Lighthouse and directs consciousness towards the work to be done.

Ritual:

1) Purify air and awaken the Enochian Light by RINGING THE BELL 9 TIMES. This signals silence and the beginning of ritual.

2) Perform the ENOCHIAN CALL to crystallize the Enochian Light's appearance and unite all participants with the atmosphere.

3) Upon finishing the Enochian Call, declare that the ENOCHIAN LIGHT IS OPEN.

4) Perform designated ceremony, discuss the work that needs to be done, go over business topics, set new goals, and focus direction. The Enochian Light is open to direct influence throughout the ritual and any discussions. All must resemble the ideals and identity.

5) Communion (drinking of soma) by acting the part of the god/goddess, take on its nature, reaching a level of divinity.

6) Upon finishing the ceremony, if any specific requests are to be read, the priest reads them out loud to the Enochian Light and then burns the parchment it was wrote on as all participants use their imagination to visualize the request as already being accomplished. Place the desire into the Unmanifest while the ether is open.

7) All participants collectively CLOSE THE ENOCHIAN LIGHT, dissipating the energy and allowing the Enochian Light to do its work in the spiritual realm. This "closing" reverses the process, allowing consciousness to return back to the roles of their ordinary

lives without rupturing their connection with the Lighthouse.

8) Reapply the 7 Holy Accessories. The priest finishes the ceremony by ringing the bell 9 times.

Enochian Call (Invocation)

"Enochian Call" is the verbal symbol that connects all members in that time / place where the ritual is being performed. First act is to consciously set one's Self apart from the laws of the universe in order to directly communicate with the Enochian Light. Next step is actual communication with the Enochian Light as an independent being.

(Begin the Enochian Call by practice of Aromatherapy, passing oil around the congregation counter - clockwise)

Anthropos, the Christos Yeshua, the Son of
Man and Son of God!
Open wide the fourth dimensional gates,
and bring forth your Fallen Angels,
thee embodiment of Light and Wisdom!

Thoth! - Hermes! - Enoch! - acknowledge
this sacred gathering!
We take these tools of Enoch within our
hands to build the
righteous temple of man. We use thee
Enochian Light to shine bright,
blinding this Age of Mass Consumerism
from our sight!
We arm ourselves with the skills and spells
necessary to navigate

through the labyrinth of illusions.
Let the metaphorical and metaphysical
become one in the Ether,
causing the body to unite everything that is
grand and scientific
in the religious dreams of the illuminated.

HAIL ENOCH!

Oh, my dearly departed loved ones -
I call upon thee to watch over us.
Provide us your strength and guidance.
Thy spirit continues.

Oh, Enochian Light -
I call upon thee to watch over us.
For protection and perfection.
Deliver us from ignorance and false
prophets!

(Priest reads the 8th Enochian Key)

Note my fails, and my success!
Heart and Mind, through you I'm blessed!
Thy soul shines, Enochian Light
A perfect god, thus All is Right!

(Priest is handed the Enochian Pipe)

"Through wisdom a house is built,
And by understandings it is established;
By knowledge the rooms are filled with all precious riches.
A wise man is strong, yes,
a man of knowledge increases strength."
(Proverbs 24: 3-5)

Thank you for watching over this congregation.
For Knowledge, Health and Wealth!

(Perform the Call to the Elements)

(Priest smokes from the Enochian Pipe and passes it around the congregation, counter-clockwise)

THE ENOCHIAN LIGHT IS OPEN!

Closing of the Enochian Light

By the grace of Enoch, we are anointed under the 63rd order.
The Last True Order, the Temple of Enochian Light.
We have walked through the Black Flame
....
Now let us exit illuminated.
By all of the sacred logos, we show the

sign. Let us be one with our Good
Demon,
the baptist of wisdom.
To those without veil-

HAIL ENOCH!
So it is done…
Be at home.

Daily Prayer

I am my Father, who art in heaven,
as I dwell upon this Earth.
Each is Christ, the All is Nature.
Thee Prince of Darkness, the star of each.
Each of us, a star - shine bright!
Thy glory is mine, My glory is yours - Love one another.
Thy Kingdom is upon us, the Time is here,
Now is the space!
Banish thou Illusion - Destroy thy Maya.
For humanity has suffered long enough ...
God feels the tears, as Lucifer drinks,
and two old friends re-unite!
Put our past antagonisms behind us!
As life is a blessing to be enjoyed,
Passion is a desire to be indulged.
Let us commune with all of humanity,
in a manner of Peace, Love, and Harmony.
Be at Home.

Psalms 82: 3- 8

Defend the poor and fatherless;
do justice to the afflicted and needy.
Deliver the poor and needy;
free them from the hand of the wicked.
They do not know, nor do they understand;
they walk about in darkness;
all the foundations of the earth are unstable.
I said, "You are gods,
and all of you are children of the Most High.
But you shall die like men,
and fall like one of the princes."
Arise, O God, judge the earth;
for You shall inherit all nations.

Holidays

Holidays are the consecrated periods of time when life throughout the cosmos must come together, celebrating unity, harmony, and the holiday's designated purpose. Each holiday has a formal ceremony, followed by a feast and a "Projection of Unified Consciousness" (in which all members are to watch a certain film documentary at the same time, meditating on the message, thus, uniting all in the spiritual realm). Through video, all participate in a shared ritual because the sound and image opens portals within the body, and meditating on the message aligns each psyche into a collective focus of purpose. When all members meditate on the same message at the same time, we are brought spiritually together - though our physical bodies are in different locations.
* Projection of Unified Consciousness is the required aspect of an Enochian holiday. This applies to all holidays except for one's own birthday and Commercial holiday celebrations.

- One's birthday (Most Important!)
- All cultural / conventional commercial holidays
- Zodiac festival (every transition of sun's position)
- Every full moon

- Valentine's Day
- The Days of Enki (10 - day festival beginning every March 22nd)
- The Feast of Crowley (3- day event ... April 8th,9th and 10th)
- Walpurgisnacht (April 30th)
- St. John the Baptist Day (June 24th)
- The 4th of July (celebration of freedom)
- August 31 - (preliminary celebration to yearly cleanse)
- September 11th (day of defiance against Holy Wars)
- All Hallow's Eve (Halloween)

Holy Pantheon

Hagiographies

- John the Baptist -"The Mysteries of John the Baptist" Tobias Churton
- Simon the Magus - "Simon Magus: The Gnostic Magician" G. R. S. Mead
- Yeshua the Christ – "Jesus the Magician" Morton Smith
- John Dee - "John Dee and The Empire of Angels" Jason louv
- Marquis de Sade - "The Marquis de Sade" Donald Thomas.
- Adam Weishaupt - "Perfectibilists" Terry Melanson
- Charles Darwin - "Autobiography of Charles Darwin" Charles Darwin
- Friedrich Nietzsche- "Nietzsche: Philosopher, Psychologist, Antichrist" Walter Kauffman
- Carl Jung - "Memories, Dream, Reflections" Carl Jung
- Aleister Crowley - "Do what Thou Wilt" Lawrence Sutin
- Ayn Rand – "We The Living" Ayn Rand
- Anton LaVey - "The Secret life of a Satanist" Blanche Barton

Canon

- “Think And Grow Rich” Napolean Hill
- “The 7 Habits of Highly Effective People” Steven Covey
- “Lords of the Left Hand Path” Stephen Flowers
- “The Satanic Scriptures” Peter H. Gilmore
- “In An Unspoken Voice” Paul Levine
- “ADHD and the Edison Gene” Thomas Hartman
- “The Lucifer Principle” Howard Bloom
- “Mind War” Michael Aquino
- “Capitalism: The Unknown Ideal” Ayn Rand
- “The 48 Laws of Power" Robert Greene
- “Inside a Magical Lodge” John Michael Greer
- “Energy Magick of the Vampyre” Don Webb

Conclusion

The universe is full of mysteries - mysteries that have been deliberately concealed from the masses since having been discovered. These mysteries are divine secrets that cannot be passed through any form of language or book. Divinity is found by following a set of thorough initiation practices that require discipline, sacrifice, brutal honesty, and a sincere desire for truth. No school of religion can teach (or sell) these secrets but The Temple of Enochian Light provides methods of "discovering"- a discovery that each man must uncover for himself. Every life is a spiritual journey, every life is RELIGIOUS! There is no pause or breaks from religion as there is no pause on life. LIFE IS RELIGION, all else is error!

Throughout the journey of life one will either lose themself to the world of illusion (lose the soul to "non-existence") or one will dedicate thy life to divinity, discover the hidden matrix, and redeem "continuance". The choice is ultimately up to each individual. Enoch has provided the spiritual direction and protection to the initiates who are in search of enlightenment and happiness!

Welcome - to a Temple wherein man and woman are free to celebrate and worship their own personal divinity ... as man is God, God is Man and the World is His Kingdom!

www.ingramcontent.com/pod-product-compliance
Ingram Content Group UK Ltd
Pitfield, Milton Keynes, MK11 3LW, UK
UKHW021932190726
13853UKWH00004B/140

9 798990 950405